THE LITTLE TERROR
Good Sleeping Guide

Charlotte Preston, RH

GW00320313

For Alfie, Sophie, Tilly, Theo, Emilio and Sofia

First published in Great Britain in 1998 by Metro Books
(an imprint of Metro Publishing Limited), 19 Gerrard Street, London W1V 7LA

Text © 1998 Charlotte Preston and Trevor Dunton
Illustrations © 1998 Trevor Dunton

Charlotte Preston and Trevor Dunton are hereby identified as the authors of this work in
accordance with Section 77 of the Copyright, Designs and Patents Act 1988.

British Library Cataloguing in Publication Data.
A CIP record of this book is available on request from the British Library.

ISBN 1 900512 23 8

10 9 8 7 6 5 4 3 2 1

Designed by Mick Keates
Typesetting and formatting by Concise Artisans
Printed in Italy by LEGO

An extra bit for parents with girls
You'll find that throughout the Little Terror books we refer to babies as 'he'.
Please don't think we've neglected your daughters, it's purely in the interests of clarity and
space. Using he/she, him/her, himself/herself is cumbersome to read and uses valuable space
that we wanted to devote to more useful topics. So, please read 'she' for 'he'.

CONTENTS

This book is about helping you, and Little Terror, to get a good night's sleep

SO WHAT'S THE SECRET ?

1. *Getting LT into good sleeping habits from the start,* or

2. *If he is not sleeping, making changes so that he learns how to go to sleep and stay asleep when **you** want him to.*

One important thing to make clear straight away is that there is no such thing as a typical baby. They're all different – different personalities and different sleep patterns – some get into a routine quickly, others take a lot longer.

If your Little Terror is one of those that never seems to sleep and, as he grows, races around with all the energy of a major volcanic eruption, you never know, he might grow into a really mellow teenager.

NEWBORN TO THREE MONTHS

So here you are, at home with your brand new Little Terror. Life will never be the same again! Don't expect too much sleep in the first month or two as he might want feeding several times a night.

His every waking moment will be spent with you: feeding, winding, nursing, nappy-changing, bathing, singing, making up bad rhymes and cuddling. It's all part of the process of bonding, while you and Little Terror get to know each other.

Well, that sounds great for LT, constant room service, but what about his parents? You're probably still reeling from the birth, and if your baby screams the second you put him down, how do you even go to the loo?

If this sounds familiar, don't worry, it won't last for ever and within a few weeks you'll be getting big, beaming smiles and

realise that you are the most special people on Earth. Meanwhile, what do you do if your LT just won't sleep? How do you look after yourself, and what can you do to help LT get into good habits?

CHECK LIST

Things to check if LT won't sleep.

1. Does he have a nappyful and need changing?

2. Is he hungry?
   Babies won't sleep if they need feeding. In the early days, most babies like feeding little and often. They love the comfort of it and, remember, they only have small tummies.

8

3 Try winding him.

Position A

Hold him upright, facing you, with his head over your shoulder, and rub his back.

Position B

Sit LT on your knee, with his legs across your lap. Hold him under his arms with one hand and rub his back with the other. In many cultures they don't 'wind' their babies at all and, if it doesn't seem to do the trick, try giving him some gripe water before feeds, or cooled, boiled water or fennel drink afterwards, which sometimes works.

A bit about wind

If he has wind, he may be guzzling his milk too fast and taking in air. Perhaps the hole in the bottle teat is too big or small, or your breast milk is gushing out (take him off the breast until it slows down by inserting your little finger into the corner of his mouth and gently removing the nipple). Don't worry if you can't seem to pinpoint the cause. Some babies are just plain windy and don't seem to improve until they get on to solids.

4 Is he too hot or too cold? He's not very good at regulating his own temperature yet, so he's sensitive to changes.

5 Is his bedroom too light? Close his curtains, or try using a night-light.

6 Is his feed too strong? If you are bottle-feeding, make sure you put the powder in the bottle after the warmed, boiled water. If you do it the other way around, you can't judge how much water you're adding and risk making the milk up too strong.

Note: *Never add extra formula to the bottle in the hope it will help LT sleep. The feed will be too concentrated, and bad for his immature kidneys.*

11

7 Does he need a reassuring cuddle? Even babies have bad days.

8 Is he unwell? Look out for the following: he won't take his feeds; he's hot and sweaty; vomiting; diarrhoea; he's floppy. If any of these symptoms persist, see your GP.

9 If you've checked all the above, try leaving him in his cot for five minutes. If he's still screaming the second you put him down, you're probably getting a bit frazzled. Give yourself a break. It won't do LT any harm to be left to cry in his cot for five minutes. It will help you to deal with the situation more rationally and, you never know, he might just relax and fall asleep.

SURVIVAL TIPS

*LT needs you fit and well. Here are a few tips
to help you hang on to your health . . .
and your marbles.*

🐑 Sleep – get it where you can!
Sleep whenever LT sleeps.

🐑 Be realistic about
what to expect. You
are unlikely to feel up
to very much at the

beginning. In fact, it's normal to be pretty much at
the end of your tether for a while.

🐑 Don't blame yourself, or LT. If LT is doing
a lot of serious bawling and not sleeping,
it might just be the way he is at the moment.
It will change. You can only do your best.

13

🐑 Leave him in his cot for five minutes and have a break. See checklist (page 12).

🐑 Get as much help as you can. Close friends, relatives, family... don't be picky, exploit them all. They can save your sanity. If you're offered help, accept it. It could just be some help with the shopping or holding LT while you have a bath.

🐑 If you don't have anyone to call on, join a mother and toddler group (ask at your baby clinic). At least you'll realise you're not alone.

🐑 **Housework? Forget it!** Home cooking? It takes time and energy and nobody will die from eating convenience foods for a while! Forget, too, about polishing and spring cleaning. If you have any energy or time left after caring for LT, spend it on yourselves.

🐑 **Timed pushing of the pushchair.** Try putting LT in a pram or pushchair after you have fed, winded and changed him. Then push him back and forwards for as long as it takes to get him settled or asleep. It's a good idea to time it to see your progress. On the first day it might take thirty minutes, but by day seven, it might only take ten.

TIK TIK

HEY! DRIVER! DOESN'T THIS THING GO ANY FASTER?

🐑 **Cuddles for everyone.** Loads of hugs and cuddles for Mum, Dad and LT – it gets rid of stress and makes everyone feel secure and loved.

GETTING INTO GOOD HABITS

The name of the game at this age is survival, but there's one thing you can do right from the start to help build good habits.

🐑 Help LT to fall asleep on his own. Once a day, make sure that he doesn't go to sleep on the bottle or breast, or while being carried around. When he looks sleepy put him into his crib, pram or pushchair. To start with you will have to rock him, sing to him or push him. LT might take time to settle, but you will be teaching him to feel secure without physical contact with you all the time.

CHECKLIST
FIRST 3 MONTHS
1. Check Nappy
2. Is LT hungry or his feeds too Strong?
3. Is LT windy?
4. Too hot or too Cold?
5. Bedroom too light?
6. Is LT unwell
7. Reassuring cuddle
8. Put in cot for 5 mins
SURVIVAL GUIDE
1. Sleep when LT sleeps
2. Be realistic
3. Remember it's not your fault
4. Get help!
5. Forget housework
6. Timed pushing of the pushchair
7 Lots more cuddles
GOOD HABITS
1. Put LT awake in crib once a day

Expect sudden growth spurts

THREE TO SIX MONTHS

At three months, babies all have very individual sleeping habits but, as he's awake for longer and longer, it's time to start easing LT into some sort of routine. Get it right now and, hopefully, you'll get away without too many bags under your eyes in the months to come.

If you are very lucky, your LT will already be sleeping like an angel until his one, regular, night-time feed and then falling fast asleep immediately afterwards.

If you're not so lucky, you may find he's waking up and feeding intermittently all night, with only short sleeps in between. Most parents' experience is somewhere in the middle, and you'll probably find that things vary as he goes through changes and growth spurts.

LT'S sleeping arrangements

Which room?
Most parents want LT with them in their bedroom for the first three months to keep an eye on him and to make night feeding easier. After that, it's a matter of personal choice. Many babies sleep

perfectly happily in their parents' room until they are well over six months. If LT is having sleep problems, don't be tempted to move him into another room. It is probably better to keep him with you until he is over six months old.

Basket, crib, cot or what?
If he's been in a cot from the start, that's great – just carry on. Otherwise, as he's growing so fast, you might like to consider moving him into a cot now.

In-cot entertainment
It's good to have one or two soft toys at the bottom of the cot. Mobiles are fine too, but beware of over-using the musical type. Your LT could start to rely on it as the trigger for sleep, and it probably won't thrill you to play 'Baa Baa Black Sheep' at three o'clock every morning.

A bit about cot death

Every parent's nightmare. Exactly why cot deaths occur is still
a mystery. Thankfully, though, the chances of it happening
are very small. Here are a few simple precautions you
can take to minimise the risks.

Avoid overheating

Pillows, duvets or cot bumpers
are not recommended at this age.
He could become trapped under
a hot duvet, or he might push his
head against the bumper, which
would keep the heat in like a hat.
If your house is reasonably warm,
use cotton blankets until he is
eighteen months. By then he will be
more active and able to move
himself away from a duvet or cot
bumper. It is probably not a good

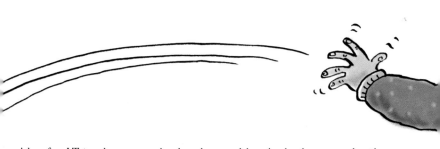

idea for LT to share your bed as he could wriggle down under the covers when you are asleep and get too hot.

Avoid contact with cigarette smoke
Smoking has been linked with cot death so don't allow LT anywhere near it.

Sleeping position
The current recommendation is that you put LT to sleep on his back. Since people have been following this advice, there has been a significant reduction in the number of cot deaths. Put him on his back with his feet against the bottom of the cot so that he cannot work his way down.

CHECK LIST

You're exhausted and LT just won't settle. What can you do about it? Get into a routine of checking the following things – they can all stop him sleeping.

1. See newborn to three months checklist (page 17).

2. If bottle-feeding and he's still hungry. The formula designed for hungrier babies might help. Start at about four months.

24

3 Is he ready for solids? Solids stay in LT's stomach for longer, so he won't have that empty feeling quite so quickly! Start from four months.

4 If all else fails, check with your health visitor or GP that there is nothing physically wrong with him.

SURVIVAL TIPS

🐑 Losing your rag? Remember it's OK to leave him crying in his cot for five minutes while you make a cup of tea and try to relax.

🐑 Get out of the house. Even if it's only for ten minutes, it helps you keep a sense of perspective. Meet other mums and share your experiences with them.

🐑 Take up all offers of help.

🐑 Don't forget to eat. Food will keep your energy and your morale up.

GETTING INTO GOOD HABITS

This section is designed to prevent problems before they happen, or resolve those you are already having.

Moooooon Riverrrrr ♪

🐑 Have a quiet time for half an hour before bedtime.

🐑 When LT is sleepy, try putting him in his cot or pushchair, still awake, once or twice a day. He might cry at first, so sing something soothing, or gently pat him.

🐑 If LT wakes in the night, no fun and games, or he'll decide waking up is great. Feed him, change him, then straight back to sleep – and you, too, hopefully.

🐑 Continue the timed pushing of the pram or pushchair (page 15) once or twice a day for about fifteen minutes. This is useful for settling LT, and a good job for Dad or a friend.

SIX TO TWELVE MONTHS

This is the age to really concentrate on getting LT into good sleeping habits.

Ideally, at six months you will begin to work towards a regular bedtime routine, i.e.:

1 tea, 2 quiet time, 3 bath, 4 bed – at the same time each day.

The routine will help him feel secure, so it's important not to let it slip.

bath

quiet time

tea

bed

Now he's much more active, bedtime becomes a major feature of the day, so try to make it something to look forward to: a lovely time, when you and LT can get close and wind down together. The key is to use positive encouragement to get LT to do what you want him to.

On the other hand, LT may not be in any sort of routine, may resist going to bed and want constant midnight feasts. He might demand to sleep in your bed and nap on top of you at any time during the day or night – it's enough to make you feel like screaming.

SLEEP DIARY

WEEK STARTING	MON	TUES	WEDS	THURS	FRI	SAT	SUN
TIME WOKE IN MORNING							
TIME PUT DOWN FOR NAP(s) IN DAY							
TIME WENT TO SLEEP FOR NAP(s) IN DAY							
TIME WENT TO BED IN EVENING							
TIME WENT TO SLEEP IN EVENING							
TIME(s) WOKE AT NIGHT							
WHAT YOU DID							
TIME(s) WENT TO SLEEP AGAIN							

If this is you, and you're feeling at the end of your tether, DON'T PANIC. You can change things, and it's important for both you and LT that you break these habits now. There's a sleep diary opposite for you to copy and fill in. It will help you to identify LT's sleep patterns and give you a clearer idea of what is happening so you can do something about it. Use the checklists to make sure there's nothing stopping LT from sleeping, then have a look at the GOOD HABITS advice on page 39 to see what changes you can make.

CHECK LIST

1 **Check the basics:** Hungry? See three to six months checklist (page 24).

2 Use the sleep diary (page 32) to keep a record of haw much LT sleeps in the day, what time he goes up to bed, when he falls asleep and his pattern of waking at night. It may help you to see what's going on.

3 **Painful teething?** This could well be the reason he's not sleeping. Some babies don't seem bothered by teething; others are very fretful.

Look for – swollen, red gums where the tooth is coming through; red cheeks; high temperature and runny poo.

To relieve the symptoms – give him baby paracetamol (Capol, or equivalent), which should soothe the pain and lower his temperature. Rubbing his gums with your fingers or using a teething ring or a teething gel can be a comfort to sore gums. If he has a sore bottom, soothe with a cream.

4 Can't get himself to sleep?
If LT wakes and won't sleep whenever you transfer him to his cot from the car/ pushchair/sofa/floor/breast or bottle, he needs to learn to go to sleep on his own in his cot. Check out the step-by-step method on page 39.

SURVIVAL TIPS

Looking after yourselves.

See three to six months SURVIVAL TIPS.

🐑 **Take time for yourselves.** Now that LT is over six months, hopefully you have recovered from his birth and will have a little more time for yourselves. Try to get out on your own by taking it in turns every other week. Your relationship is important, so why not arrange a babysitter once a month? Now is the time to ask family or friends to help or join a babysitting circle.

🐑 **Meet other humans.** Look for activities where you can meet other parents.

If you can find one with a crèche so LT will be looked after for a time, even better!

Some are free or just make a nominal charge – try swimming, for example. Other activities include baby gyms for LT, keep-fit for mum and mother and toddler groups where parents with young children can meet.

🐑 **Go to bed as early as you need.** Don't be surprised if you can't stay awake past 9pm!

🐑 If you're looking after LT full-time, do at least one thing a week completely for yourself. It'll do you the world of good. Swimming, keep-fit, an evening class, or just going out with a good mate or your mum. Of course, LT's wonderful, but getting a bit of space between you for a while will help you appreciate him even more.

🐑 If you're going out to work, it's just as important to find space in the week for yourself. Doing two jobs is going to be very demanding, but if you can find the time, you'll feel the benefit.

GETTING INTO GOOD HABITS

The 'step-by-step' method – teaching him to fall asleep on his own.

This approach helps LT to feel safe and loved while he gradually changes his trigger for going to sleep from you to himself and learns to drop off to sleep on his own. Start during the day. It will be easier than trying to teach LT new tricks at night when you're exhausted.

Before you start

Begin filling in the sleep diary a week before you start and continue until you have achieved your goal. The diary will help you follow what's happening (see page 32).

Step 1

Check your sleep diary to find the time when LT usually falls asleep in the day, put him in his cot about ten minutes before this time and stay very close to him until he goes to sleep, soothing him by patting and singing. It could take up to an hour and, as long as he is not particularly upset, it's worth sitting it out.

If, on the other hand, it is obvious that he is not going to settle and he is upset, take him out of the cot after fifteen minutes, let him calm down and, when he looks sleepy, repeat the process until he drops off. At first, as he is learning to go to sleep on his own, you might have to repeat this several times.

When you've calmed him down, he might want to fall asleep in your arms or on the sofa – don't let him. Put him back in his cot, repeating the process until he finally settles.

Step 2
Once he's used to settling in his cot, instead of patting and singing to him, try sitting on a chair very close, with just your hand on him. Stay there until he's asleep. (You are starting to reduce your attention.)

Step 3

After one week, start moving your chair away, about a foot every three days, until you are near the door.

Step 4

When he is settling in his cot with you sitting on the chair by the door, start nipping out and coming back. Initially for about ten seconds, then very gradually increasing the time you are out. The whole process could take two or three weeks, or less (with a bit of luck).

Teaching LT when to go to sleep

Once he has learned how to go to sleep, it's time to show him
when. To prevent day-time naps interfering with night-time sleep,
they should be between 10.00am and 3.30pm.

Put him down to sleep at about the same time each day.
Use the same principle when he changes from two naps a day to
one. His daytime naps will shorten as he sleeps longer at night.

If he absolutely refuses to settle, try taking him for a short walk in
the pram or pushchair. He's
more likely to drop off in
motion. When he's got
the idea of falling asleep
at the same time each
day, it's time to try him in
his cot again. If you're lucky
he'll go out like a light
immediately, but it could take up to a
couple of weeks to get him used to the idea.

Waking up at night and how to stop it

Babies, like adults, have periods of deep sleep and lighter sleep. LT will be waking up at various points during the night. If there's nothing wrong (see checklist page 8), and you're forgetting what a whole night's sleep feels like, it's about time LT was taught what night-time is for (until, that is, he starts to party).

So here goes:
Note any changes/progress in sleeping habits in your sleep diary.

1️⃣ **When LT wakes during the night**, don't reward him with midnight feasts, cuddles in your bed or playing with him, or :

🐑 He'll think it's a good idea and wake up more and more.

🐑 He won't be too pleased when you put him back in his cot.

Try to settle him using the 'step-by-step' method (page 39). This will be tiring, so if possible take turns with your partner, and keep thinking about those whole nights of sleep you'll soon be having.

2 **Whether you're bottle- or breastfeeding**, try introducing a period during the night when you don't feed at all – between midnight and 2am, for example. Gradually increase this time by fifteen minutes every third night. You might have to comfort him by other means but stick to your guns and you'll break the habit of feeds during the night. Don't worry about him going hungry. Once the night feeds are dropped, he'll eat more in the day.

3 **If you are giving LT formula milk during the night**, start watering it down by one-tenth every third night until all he is getting is water. If you give juice (not recommended as it's bad for his teeth), water it down in the same way.

TWELVE TO EIGHTEEN MONTHS

Well, you must have done something right! A year has gone by, you and your Little Terror are still here and, thanks to all your hard work, he may even be getting the hang of sleeping through the night, although 20 per cent of one-year-olds will still wake regularly at night. This is the age to firm up on techniques learnt when he was under a year. If you want to move on, go to the over-eighteen-months section.

Your once-gurgling, cuddly baby is spending less time asleep and starting to realise what his legs and arms are for. By eighteen months, he'll be running around like a maniac, discovering more and more about the world. Get ready for an exhausting and rewarding time. See six to twelve months checklist (page 34).

OVER EIGHTEEN MONTHS

Disturbed sleep?

Even if he was sleeping well before, his new-found independence might disrupt his sleep patterns. He might start waking up at night, or resist going to bed and get over-tired.

Other causes of disturbed sleep could be illness or change – e.g., new house, new baby, mum returning to work or even minor things like coming back from a visit or being on holiday.

Holidays can affect sleeping patterns

If LT's previously regular sleep patterns are disturbed, go back to the step-by-step method (page 39) for a week or two, and he should get back into his good habits again.

If, on the other hand, LT has hardly ever slept when you wanted him to, talk to your doctor or health visitor. Once you are sure that there are no medical or developmental reasons for his not sleeping, you have to assume that he just hasn't learnt how to fall asleep on his own or to sleep through the night.

If you are having problems, and feel shattered from lack of sleep, it may seem a bit overwhelming. Remind yourself that you can change things (though it will need a lot of determination), and ask your doctor or health visitor whether there's a local sleep clinic where you can get some support.

CHECK LIST

1. Use the other checklists to find out why LT is not sleeping.

2. If he's nearly two, and trying to climb out of his cot all the time, think about getting him a bed. If you are worried that he keeps getting out of bed, go back to the step-by-step method (page 39).

Time for bed

3 Is he asleep most of the day or are you trying to put him to bed too early? There's no point in starting his bedtime routine at 6pm if he isn't getting to sleep until 10pm.

4 Is he frightened of the dark? Try a night-light or leave the door open with a light on outside.

5 **Keep a sleep diary for a week**, then start his bedtime routine half an hour before he usually falls asleep. On the third night, start it fifteen minutes earlier, and every third night start another fifteen minutes earlier. Bear in mind that children, like adults, require different amounts of sleep, so bedtimes will vary.

6 **Does he feel he is missing the fun when he is in bed?** Keep the noise down until he's asleep.

SURVIVAL TIPS

Though babies' sleeping arrangements vary widely between families and cultures, none is better or worse. The only important thing is that your LT is fitting in with your life and doing what you want. The younger he learns how, when and where **you** want him to go to sleep the better. You might crack it in his first year, it could take longer. If he's not doing what you want, you have to make the changes, because LT won't change on his own. If you're having difficulties remember you're not alone. Roughly a third of pre-school children have sleep problems.

🐑 **Set a date** for starting the step-by-step plan and work at it with your partner.

🐑 **Look after yourself** (see page 36). Try finding a playgroup or nursery for LT so that you can have a bit of free time for yourself.

🐑 **The local library** is a good source of information.

GETTING INTO GOOD HABITS

Breaking bad habits – bribery, deception and the 'No Attention' method.

LT can now run rings round you and talk the hind legs off a donkey. He can also get out of bed easily. If he's about two and you can't stop him waking or getting out of bed at night, a mixture of encouragement, bribery and deception might do the trick:

Be kind but firm. Let him know you mean what you say. Don't give him rewards for coming into your bed – take him straight back to his cot and no messing. Set a limit on bedtime stories. Don't give in to requests for 'just one more'.

Give a lot of positive encouragement if he's doing well.

If LT is waking early, make sure he has some toys in his cot to play with. If he's waking horribly early when he's older, say 3am or 4am, you'll have to use a little deception. Give him an alarm clock (or use a timer on the light switch) and tell him he can come into your room when it goes off (or comes on). Set it at the time he usually wakes for the first three mornings, then move it forwards by fifteen minutes every third day.

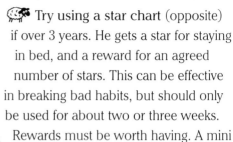

🐑 Try using a star chart (opposite) if over 3 years. He gets a star for staying in bed, and a reward for an agreed number of stars. This can be effective in breaking bad habits, but should only be used for about two or three weeks. Rewards must be worth having. A mini packet of sweets, dried fruit or other small treats, whatever feels right.

🐑 If you haven't managed to get LT to sleep through the night, the 'No Attention' approach is probably worth a try (see page 63). This is based on not rewarding him with attention for waking up, or for not going to sleep in the first place. Only you can judge when the 'No Attention' approach is appropriate, or whether to use it at all. It can be very effective as early as a year, and if you are desperate to sleep, it's worth trying.

Many parents worry that leaving LT to cry might do him permanent harm, and certainly a baby under six months should not

STAR CHART

	WEEK 1		WEEK 2		WEEK 3	
MONDAY	⭐		⭐		⭐	
TUESDAY	☆		☆		⭐	
WEDNESDAY	⭐		⭐		☆	
THURSDAY	☆		⭐		⭐	
FRIDAY	⭐	TREAT	☆		⭐	
SATURDAY	☆		⭐	TREAT	⭐	
SUNDAY	☆		☆		⭐	TREAT

COLOUR IN A STAR IF LT STAYS IN HIS BED ALL NIGHT

THREE STARS IN WEEK 1 = TREAT
FOUR STARS IN WEEK 2 = TREAT
SIX STARS IN WEEK 3 = TREAT

be left to cry for any length of time. After that, it should only be used as a way of helping him sleep. But, be reassured, this is a method used by many child psychologists to break the cycle of children not sleeping.

If it seems a bit harsh to you, there's a slightly gentler version where you check every five minutes and just tell him to go back to sleep, but this will take longer.

If it's a struggle, try to imagine what a relief it will be when LT eventually sleeps through the night and you can start getting your life back to normal again. You'll also have more energy for LT during the day.

The 'No Attention' approach

Make sure LT is well and there is no emotional reason he is not sleeping. When he wakes at night, don't go in to him.

If, on the first night, you cannot stand the screaming (it might go on for over an hour) check him every five minutes to start with, then every ten minutes, though bear in mind this checking could start him off again.

This method can be upsetting for you, but if you've tried everything else and you're desperate, it usually works. If you don't go in to him at all, LT should be sleeping through in less than a week. The checking method will take longer, but there's nothing wrong with going in to reassure yourself that he's OK when it all goes quiet. It's better than lying there worrying about it!

If you've tried all this and LT's still having difficulty sleeping, you'll need some extra support. Ask your health visitor to check the national sleep clinic register to see if there's one in your area. If not, your GP or health visitor should be able to give you support in identifying and solving the problem.

If LT's awake, everyone's awake, and you're all going to be tired and irritable. We hope that this book has helped you get LT into good habits, and given you ways to deal with the problems that crop up. It's important to get it right now, as most older children who are poor sleepers had sleep problems as babies. Your well-being is crucial to LT's, and he wants you to be the kind of happy, smiley parents you get in adverts. You'll need plenty of rest for that, so sleep tight.